POETRY HOES

Ridhima Sharma

ISBN 978-93-5610-497-6

Published in India 2022 by Pencil

A brand of
One Point Six Technologies Pvt. Ltd.
123, Building J2, Shram Seva Premises,
Wadala Truck Terminal, Wadala (E)
Mumbai 400037, Maharashtra, INDIA
E connect@thepencilapp.com
W www.thepencilapp.com

Author biography

Hey, My sugarplums

I am all about expressing yourselves through some creative medium, be it poetry or any other Art. Consider this your friend who knows that at times you might feel sad, depressed, or lonely. Lemme tell you it's all normal. Trust me, not many people would tell you this but craving someone is human. Virtual hugs to all those who don't feel lovable, know that someone out there is definitely craving your presence and vibes. At times, when you feel like having a mental breakdown session, do it! Have a good cry! But don't cry over it twice! Your next step is to grab your favorite beverage, a pen, and your favorite diary. Pen down all your heartfelt good and bad emotions in poetry. Or have a taste of this book babies! Dive into a sexy drive!

XOXO
RIDHIMA SHARMA

CONTENTS

Those 'Intimacy' Shots

While nothing makes me happy
I seek shots of 'Intimacy'
I seek it with a lie
and cheers happen with my person pouring a 'goodbye'

And with every shot, I sought a lie
I see the fake smile
with a clear eye
Those 'Intimacy shots'
have after sodas
in 'midnight cries'
and mornings of numb eyes

Drunk and drowning in
Those 'Intimacy' shots

ONE GLASS OF 'ATTENTION' SIR!

Can I have a sip of your 'lust'!

I smell deep arousal of lust
while my eyes shut
slowly burning
the desire of painting my soul once

My body acting as 'canvas' for you
while you pour your cajole lust
all over my soft bones

Hey, can I be your slut
I want you on the edges and curves
I want your fingertips
doing a slow dance
on my nerves

Now,
I might need two sips of your 'Lust'

Worship my 'Lips' Till I lose my breath

I heard you hate my voice
why don't you curse it with
your lips
on my berry 'nude' lipstick?

Passion in your sin
and blood dripping on my abused lip
slowly I swallow it like
blood and butter
inside, with a luscious sigh!

Look, Pin me against the wall
Wait, Let me choke a little more
Let me be the fragrant taste your mouth desires
and taste me
till I 'lose my breath'!

Your 'touch' is what i 'crave'

I need those 'chills' of your touch
but all I'm getting are those 'shivers' of lost hopes
I wonder if you ever will crave
my soul again!
and grab me
while chasing my taste!

I want the color of my skin red
iron in my blood is dead
slowly your fingers all over my chest
only the lust knows where things might end

You, and I
and those cravings which never end!

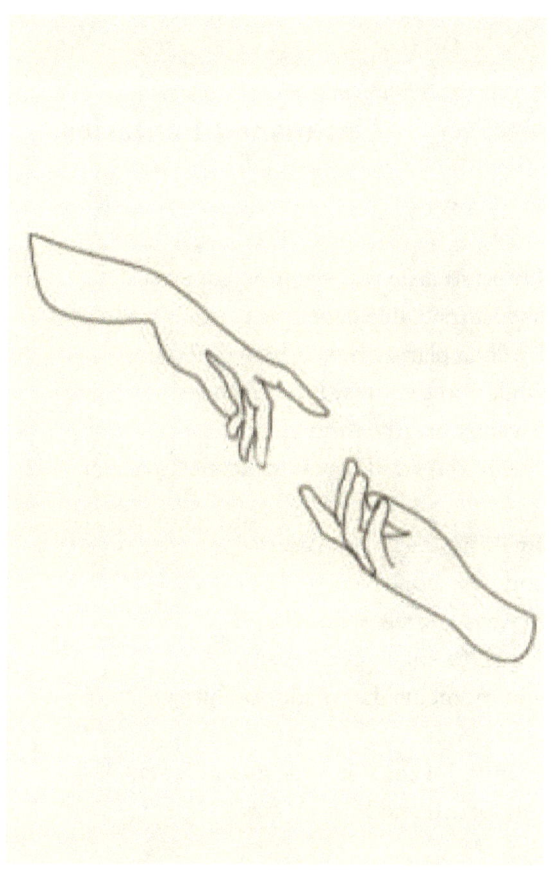

Unfinished Fantasies

I want to taste that scent on your neck
like a drug while having sex
I wanna play with your hair a Lil more
while you can't resist me anymore
I wanna breathe through you
slowly and steadily you make me 'love you'

I wish to touch your bruises
and your bones
in ways entirely seductive
I wish to know every scar
and moments that made you bizarre

Honey, I wanna be your unsaid fantasy
untouched and high on cum!

Dark Confession

steamy sex, a sucker for hot baths
subtle steps closer to your heart
treat me like a piece of art
paint my wild side
until the sunrise

soft echo
my mouth does
while you fix that void in my heart, neck, and parts nobody knows
I swallow all your sorrows, deep inside those cuddles
In your darkest thoughts, let me hustle
let me be your sin once

Let me be your whore
i hate being the 'girl next door' anymore!

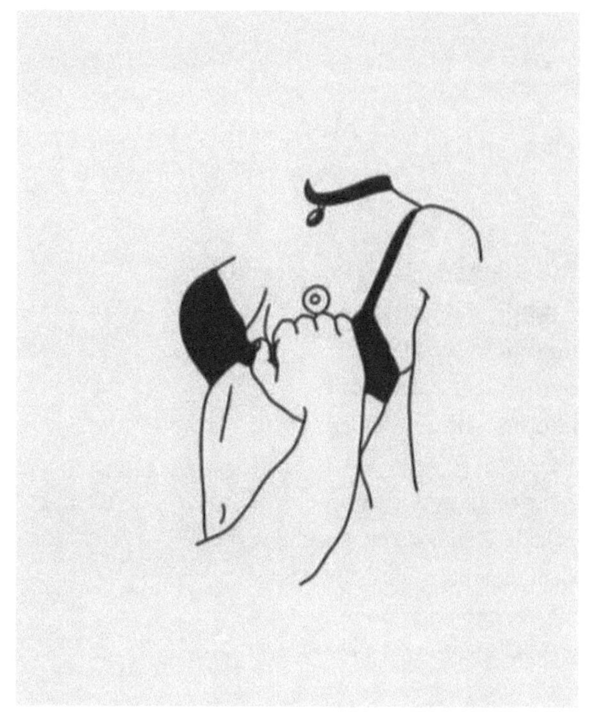

Holy Hickey !

Are you ready for the impressions
I slowly and passionately
imprint on your neck
on two soft collar bones
into the saliva, in blurry nights

Are you getting that urge of tattoos,
honey, let me show you the real ones
with cigarettes and slow kisses
inhale, exhale, infinite, steamy
waves of smooches to ink you pretty

While you shout
and I sigh
Holy Hickey!

Lurking in some lust

Saw you looking appeasing
slowly waiting pretty
scenarios building; and my head is hurting
I'm a sucker for lurking

Shy only till you saw me
standing still
but trust me, my heart is dirty

Faking my presence of emotionlessness
Do you need that seducing sense?
I ain't begging for attention
but you know
I kinda love lurking!

Touch starved

When I mention
I want you here
I want to hug you in heat of sweat
curtains downs would expect no less

Huge breath, I want to gaze at all the parts
Wrap your arms around my thighs
Kiss me slow, hitting the right note
I know we were strangers before
but,
leave now no stone

let me unfold your mysteries

lets blindfold for a moment
pull me over, feel my movement
ill put on my summer dress, wild and bold

Grab me from the edges, put me on a desk
say that you love me,
like a naked poetry ends

Who knows if all this is a secret or a sin?
let's not repel,
before we animate a luscious scene

Turn me On

Just want those hands
seductively reaching my right spots
Falling, screaming, moaning
and u pouring sensations long-lasting

Lying that I need time
for I don't want you to stop

Smell bitter
but taste better

ah, just the fingers
forcing feelings
My heart needs you to
cut some slack honey!

What's the delay !

I got no patience
Hold me
pin me against the wall
For when i shall behold

Pretty skies
Lusty nights
Crimson days
while I slay

Run those fingers
all over my body
Darling,?
The night is young
Two of us
in the most luscious one

Gaze desperate !

I am a chaos
finding love and peace in your words
Not really sticking to that part
I assume more from your heart

Seasons of emotions
might run down my throat
but I would want you to choke me a little more

Selfishness has no heights
lemme guess
We're in desperate attempts of high tides?

www.ingramcontent.com/pod-product-compliance
Lightning Source LLC
LaVergne TN
LVHW050429160726
843469LV00041B/1294

* 9 7 8 9 3 5 6 1 0 4 9 7 6 *